ON THIS DAY!

The Holidays of the United States of America

By: Andre J. Barreto

On This Day! The Holidays of the United States of America
Written by Andre J. Barreto
Illustrated by Andre J. Barreto
Copyright © 2024 Andre J. Barreto
ISBN: 979-8-218-47623-6
Second Edition

Disclaimer: While this book provides information about American holidays and includes some historical content, it is intended for educational and entertainment purposes only. The author and publisher have made every effort to ensure the accuracy of the information presented. Any errors or omissions are unintentional.

To all children, the greatest gifts of the world.

May your days be filled with wonder, laughter, and the joy of discovery as you learn about the special holidays that make our country so unique.

New Years Day

Times Square
Manhattan, NY

On this day, we celebrate the beginning of the New Year. We celebrate New Years Day on January 1st.

HAPPY NEW YEAR!

The year is over.
That means 365 days have
passed, and now we start over
at Day 1.

Let's celebrate all the fun we had, and
cheer on the new year.

Los Angeles Skyline

MARTIN LUTHER KING JR DAY

On this day, we celebrate a great American who stood up against inequality and unfairness in America. We celebrate his good work on the 3rd Monday of January.

One day, he stood taller than any other American and reminded America to treat others fairly no matter how they look. We are all Americans.

Washington's Birthday

On this day, we celebrate the first president of the United States of America. We celebrate this day on the third Monday of February.

George Washington

George Washington led the Army to free America from Great Britain, and was very important in the making of the U.S. Constitution, the law of the land.

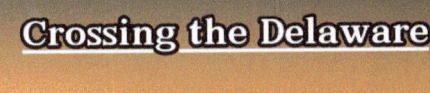

Crossing the Delaware

We the People

This day is also known as President's Day, where we celebrate all of the presidents of America.

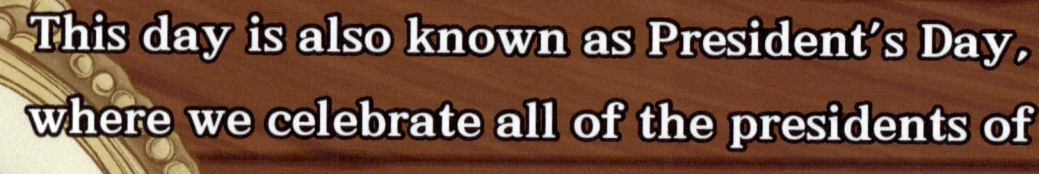

The president lives in Washington D.C.

RONALD REAGAN

BARACK OBAMA

This is the White House.
It's where the president lives.

The president is the leader of the United States of America. We, the people, pick a new president every four years.

Mount Rushmore

Memorial Day

On this day, we honor the troops who fought for the United States of America and lost their lives.

We celebrate Memorial Day on the last Monday of May.

From the Revolutionary War to the War on Terror;
we use this day to remember the people who gave
their lives for the United States of America, for
liberty, for the people, Americans like us.

Juneteenth

On this day, we celebrate the end of slavery.
We celebrate Juneteenth on June 19th.

Emancipation Oak

Abraham Lincoln
freeing the slaves

When Abraham Lincoln signed the Emancipation
Proclamation to free people from slavery, some slave
owners did not listen.

Abraham Lincoln

Abraham Lincoln is the 16th president of the United States

Abraham Lincoln led the Northern states, called the Union, in the Civil War. They fought against the Southern states, called the Confederacy, to keep our country together and end slavery.

Lincoln believed everyone should be free, and his leadership helped make that happen.

The Emancipation Proclamation was an order from President Abraham Lincoln, to make slavery illegal in the southern states.

To ensure slavery would be abolished forever in America, Lincoln worked hard to pass the 13th Amendment.

By the President of the United States of America:

A Proclamation

But, even after the 13th Amendment was passed, slave owners, in the state of Texas, did not want to free their slaves.

TEXAS

General Gordon Granger

On June 19th, Union troops, sent by the President, arrived in Galveston, Texas, to free those slaves, ending slavery in America.

INDEPENDENCE DAY

HAPPY BIRTHDAY

America's Birthday

On this day, we celebrate the birthday of our home, the United States of America.

We celebrate Independence Day on the 4th of July.

The Thirteen Colonies of Great Britain

You must pay these taxes. I am king.

Before the United States of America was born, it was the 13 American colonies of Great Britain. King George III, increased the cost of goods like paper, tea, and sugar but did not let the colonists make their own decisions about their lives.

Then the colonists created the Declaration of Independence and sent it to the king to tell him they wanted to leave Great Britain.

Declaration of Independence

Thomas Jefferson

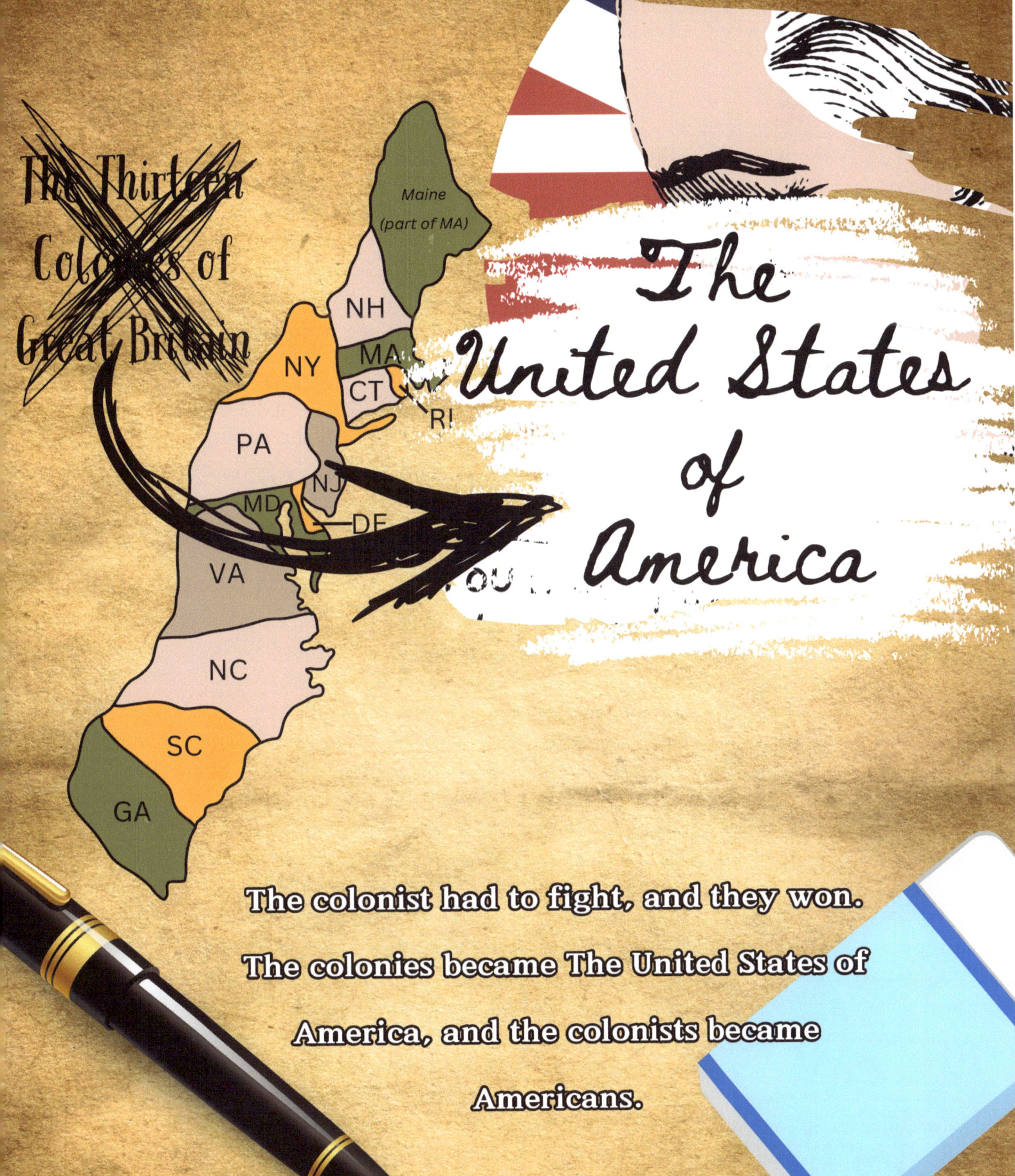

The Thirteen Colonies of Great Britain

The United States of America

The colonist had to fight, and they won. The colonies became The United States of America, and the colonists became Americans.

Labor day

On this day, we celebrate the hard work of the people of the United States of America. We celebrate Labor Day on the first Monday of September.

Construction workers build buildings and roads, farmers grow and raise food, truck drivers move goods, doctors and nurses help to heal, and first responders such as firefighters, police, and EMTs help with emergencies.

Americans, together, work hard every day to make all of our lives better.

Columbus Day

On this day, we celebrate the Italian explorer Christopher Columbus who founded America. We celebrate this day on the second Monday of October.

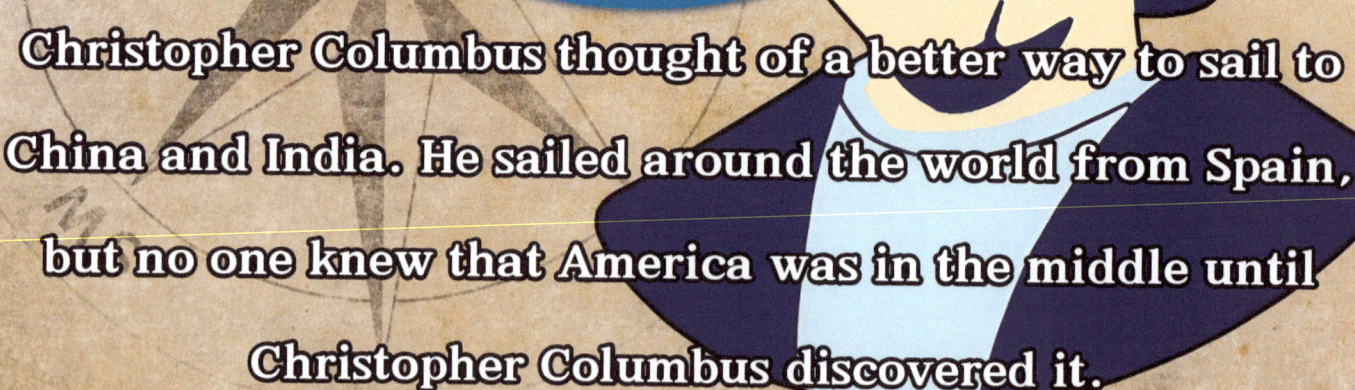

Christopher Columbus thought of a better way to sail to China and India. He sailed around the world from Spain, but no one knew that America was in the middle until Christopher Columbus discovered it.

The ships he sailed to America were named the Niña, the Pinta, and the Santa Maria. Other people wanted to explore America too and this eventually led to the United States of America being born.

Veterans Day

On this day, we celebrate our Military Veterans.

We celebrate this day on November 11th.

Our military veterans have served in the Army,

Airforce, Coast Guard, Marines, Navy, or Space Force.

They served for America and Liberty.

Veterans have fought in wars, and risked their
lives so American can remain free.

We honor and thank our veterans, all around us, for
their service to America.

Thanksgiving

On this day we give thanks for the good in our lives and celebrate with a feast. We celebrate this day on the last Thursday of November.

Don't forget to bring some food too. You can cook mashed potatoes or green bean casserole. How about sweet potato casserole?! It comes with yummy marshmallows!

Thanksgiving started when the Pilgrims sailed to America on the the Mayflower. The Native Americans taught the Pilgrims how to grow corn, catch fish, and gather berries.

The Pilgrims wanted to celebrate and give thanks for their new friends. They invited the Native Americans to join them for a feast, where they shared meals, played games, and celebrated for three days.

Christmas Day

On this day we celebrate Christmas, a day of giving, and a day to celebrate the birth of our lord and savior, Jesus Christ. We celebrate Christmas on December 25th.

Merry Christmas

Hopefully you were good this year, because Santa snuck down the chimney last night to leave us a present. Oh, and don't worry if you don't have a chimney. Santa Claus always finds a way to give you your present.

The christmas presents are under the tree! So, let's be very thankful for what we got. Don't forget that christmas is a day of giving. What gift did you give?

On Christmas we also celebrate the birth of Jesus Christ. God loves every one of us. So, god gave his son, Jesus, to show us how much he loves us, and to teach us how to love each other. God loves you, your family, your neighbors, and everyone in the world.